The Authentic Leader
Leading with Purpose and Passion

By:
Mustafa A. Nejem

Table of Contents

Chapter **01**

Discovering Your Authentic Self

Before one can begin to lead authentically, the journey inward toward self-awareness must first commence. Leading from a place of authenticity requires deep introspection in order to understand our fundamental values, purpose, and what drives us to lead. Only by peeling back the layers can we navigate life's unpredictable terrain with confidence and conviction. This chapter explores my lifelong process of self-discovery - the challenges encountered, insights gained, and continual growth that shaped me into the leader I strive to be today. My hope is that by openly sharing my experiences, readers will feel empowered and motivated in their own authentic leadership development.

Like many, my upbringing conditioned me from a young age to suppress emotions and to seek approval above all else. Coming from a traditional household where strict rules reigned, for the longest time I never felt good enough. Every accomplishment still felt mediocre in comparison to what was expected of me. The praise I craved never seemed forthcoming, leaving me riddled with self-doubt and insecurity. Outwardly I projected an image of confidence, but inside turmoil raged as I struggled to reconcile what others saw versus how I felt. It wasn't until college that I began chipping away at this facade, slowly learning to value myself unconditionally.

As a first-generation immigrant attending an elite university, imposter syndrome was a daily battle. Academically I thrived, but socially I often felt like a outsider, as if I was playing a role I wasn't meant for. To cope, I dove headfirst into extracurricular activities, taking on more responsibilities in the hopes it would fill the void of not belonging. Externally, my resume grew more impressive with each passing semester. But internally, emptiness and loneliness persisted despite a growing list of achievements.

It was only when I mustered the courage to be truly vulnerable with close friends that healing began. Their unconditional acceptance taught me that I didn't have to be perfect or what others envisioned to be worthy of love and belonging.

My transition after college into the corporate world only exacerbated feelings of inadequacy. Suddenly, I was one of the only minorities in leadership meetings as I worked my way up the ranks of a large technology company.

Microaggressions were common, whether subtle digs at my accent or presumptive comments about where I was "really" from. For the first few years, enduring such slights emerged as a daily survival task requiring Herculean effort to keep composure. Anger and frustration threatened to undo all I had built so far if not properly channeled. But through journaling, therapy, and open conversations with mentors, I cultivated emotional intelligence that allowed me to address such incidents with empathy, poise and strategic confrontation when needed.

It was during these formative years that self-awareness truly began taking shape. Through ongoing introspection and soliciting diverse outside perspectives, certain core values crystallized - values of integrity, empathy, and justice that would come to define my unique leadership approach. As I grew more secure in who I was beyond titles and achievements, external validation mattered less.

Authenticity became the compass guiding decisions large and small. I no longer feared rocking the boat when people's humanity was at stake. My leadership energy shifted from appeasing others to empowering my teams holistically so they too could thrive.

Despite significant progress, self-doubt still occasionally creeps in, a reminder of how deeply ingrained certain narratives can become. In those moments, reflecting on past crucibles provides much needed perspective. I've come to accept that leadership is an ongoing evolution requiring continual self-examination rather than a destination to reach. Lifelong learning, adapting to contextual realities, and embracing imperfections as opportunities for growth remain essential pillars for nurturing authentic presence.

Today, my leadership approach stems from bringing my whole self - joys, struggles and all - into how I show up each day. By prioritizing empathy, courageous accountability and building trust through vulnerability, diversity thrives

where once exclusion reigned. This enlightened organizational culture where people feel empowered to achieve their highest potential is my proudest accomplishment thus far.

But complacency has no place in a world undergoing constant change. As long as bias and inequity persist, the work of cultivating self-awareness and leading others authentically will never end. I've come a long way on this journey, yet farther still to travel. My hope in sharing is that others find solace in identifying principles and practices that cultivate their authentic best.

1.1 Exploring the Journey to Self-Awareness

Self-awareness lies at the heart of authentic leadership. Without truly understanding ourselves - our true motivations, inherent biases, areas for growth - it is impossible to lead from a place of integrity and bring our whole selves into the role.

However, developing self-awareness through deep introspection is no simple feat. It requires dedicated effort and openness to see beyond surface level understanding into deeper truths that may be uncomfortable to acknowledge. In this section, I explore my ongoing journey to cultivate self-awareness through sustained reflection practices, welcomed critique, and experiences that stretched my perceptions in productive ways.

From childhood, I kept much of my inner world privately locked away, focused on meeting external measures of success and approval. As a high achieving student, I defined my self-worth through grades and accomplishments rather than developing an inner compass. It was only in college that I began journaling regularly, a simple practice that eventually proved immensely valuable. At first, I mainly used it to decompress after long days or vent frustrations.

But over time, themes emerged through reflections on interpersonal dynamics, emotional reactions, and root causes for certain behaviors. In those pages, subconscious patterns and biases slowly floated to conscious realization through honest self-examination.

Journaling allowed me to look within during calm moments to gain perspective I lacked in daily life's hustle and bustle. By processing experiences from a removed angle, I recognized where insecurities influenced decisions and how certain core values consistently shaped my stance even during intense debates.

Critically reviewing my journal entries months or years later also revealed the tremendous growth that occurred without conscious effort through simple self-reflective writing. It served as a personal record of my evolving perspectives and understanding of who I was beyond performance achievements. Regular journaling became an invaluable lifelong practice for nurturing self-awareness that I still maintain today.

Along with journaling, unloading feelings and perspectives with close confidantes played a huge role in strengthening self-awareness. Through meaningful conversations where judgment was suspended, they held up mirrors reflecting truths I struggled to see alone. Their objective yet caring viewpoints challenged blindspots and assumptions, pushing me to interrogate stances from other angles outside my existing frame of reference.

Discussing everything from relationships to career pivots to social or political views exposed inherent biases through respectful discourse.

Uncomfortable feedback from confidantes also prompted a willingness to seek diverse experiences that stimulated new ways of thinking. I took risks stepping far outside my comfort zone whether working abroad in unfamiliar regions, joining activist campaigns espousing views opposed to mine, or immersing myself in communities and cultures starkly different from my own upbringing.

Each foray peeled away layers to expose deeper motivations and assumptions not evident before. They demonstrated that self-awareness is not developed through insulation but by challenging preconceived notions with openness and empathy toward perspectives radically unlike our own.

Of course, the willingness and vulnerability required for such honest self-reflection did not emerge naturally, but took dedicated mentors and support systems to cultivate. Early career missteps where emotional reactivity impacted decisions prompted self-evaluation to develop emotional intelligence.

Through therapy and executive coaching focused on behavioral change, I learned to curb knee-jerk reactions by first understanding emotional triggers beneath surface level frustrations. Pausing to gain perspective in difficult moments retrained my response patterns over time to make space for empathetic problem solving. With practice, self-control strengthened along with self-knowledge of weaknesses to continuously shore up.

The journey for self-awareness remains lifelong as new contexts create opportunities for even more growth.

Openness to constructive criticism from multiple trusted

voices prevents complacency or illusion of arrival at a final destination. Self-awareness springs from a commitment to lifelong learning through experience, introspection and a compassionate understanding of others and myself. Its prize lies not in arriving at absolute truth but in cultivating empathy, integrity and bringing my whole self into how I serve and lead with purpose. The rewards outweigh any vulnerability along this perpetual progression of self-discovery.

1.2 Overcoming Fears and Doubts to Understand Core Values/Motives

Fears are an inherent part of the human experience, developed early in life as a means of self-preservation.

However, deeply ingrained fears can also obstruct our potential if left unexamined. For years, my own persistent doubt stunted personal growth and leadership clarity as I strove to meet unrealistic standards of perfection. It was not until I mustered the courage within to directly confront these fears that transformative understanding of my true motives and values emerged. This section chronicles my ongoing journey overcoming entrenched fears and doubts to cultivate authentic leadership presence anchored by a coherent internal compass.

One core fear stemmed from an inherent sense of never measuring up ingrained from a young age. As an only child of immigrants with high expectations, I came to view any imperfection or mistake as failure. This narrative took root that others' love and acceptance depended on achievements, forcing doubts deep within a tightly controlled façade.

Perfectionism became a survival mechanism to gain approval and counter nagging inner critic. Yet underneath, insecurity and self-loathing festered from pretending infallibility while loathing inevitable shortcomings.

It was not until failing in my first managerial role that cracks in this defense surfaced. A major project fell through due harsh execution flaws on my part, laying bare vulnerabilities for all to witness. Shame overwhelmed as I expected the worst, fully anticipating demotion or firing as just consequences for imperfection. While supportive leaders recognized growth opportunities instead of failures, inner turmoil took far longer healing old wounds.

Therapy exposed roots of these narratives as adaptive during development yet maladaptive to well-being and growth as an adult. Retraining thought patterns required disciplined effort recognizing humanity in imperfection instead of condemnation.

Gradually facing perceived inadequacies head-on facilitated replacing intrinsic worth equations with self-acceptance. Rather than fearing mistakes, I learned embracing imperfection as opportunities fostering understanding and progress.

Normalizing vulnerability among colleagues encouraged experimentation without repercussions. Accepting compliments challenged dismissing achievements as worthless unless flawless. Most impactfully, sharing doubts with trusted confidantes dismantled illusion of lone survivalism by normalizing shared humanity. Their unconditional support demolished myths that worth hinged on performance alone while establishing community for mutual empowerment.

With self-esteem less contingent on upholding impossible standards, internal clarity emerged around core values and purpose. Empathy crystallized through embracing shared fragility whereas justice strengthened countering myths of personal deficiency. And service oriented purpose beyond achievements by focusing outward to uplift others however possible.

While insecurity periodically resurfaces, perspective shifts from a deficit to growth mindset recognizing evolution over destination eases residual doubts' hold. And facing fears with courage and compassion demonstrates leadership emphasizing strengths in togetherness over sole accomplishments.

Certainly, confronting stubborn fears demanded pushing far outside comfort zones into vulnerable arenas, but each challenge peeled back more masking layers. For example, publicly sharing career stumbles at industry events loosened perfectionist binds, connecting with others through admission of difficulties.

Candid conversation circles broaching taboo topics from relationships to regrets fostered discomfort familiarity reducing avoidance. Even immersing in activist campaigns confounding views stretched acceptance of divergent stances. Consistently placing myself in contexts triggering historic patterns accelerated dismantling through experience versus imagination alone.

Of course, retraining ingrained constructs remains ongoing as new contexts trigger residual fears. But increased awareness facilitates rapid recognition and assessing triggers rationally versus reactively. Building support networks normalizing shared imperfections provides community countering isolationism. And consciously anchoring purpose and decisions to coherent values rooted in serving others beyond self-interests maintains clear leadership identity amid doubts.

While absolute conquering of fears proves unrealistic, leadership maturity emerges through compassionately facing fears however they appear instead of pretending invincibility.

In fostering empathy through shared vulnerability, authentic connections empower far beyond what any achievement alone could provide.

1.3 Examining how life experiences shape leadership approach

Our life histories comprising countless unique experiences, relationships, challenges, and opportunities profoundly influence the leaders we become. For me, various defining moments along the journey reshaped understanding of effective leadership in impactful ways.

Through adversity arose clarity, toughened resolve found fresh purpose, and human connection salvaged direction. This section chronicles transformative periods elevating self-awareness by examining how key life lessons molded my ongoing leadership approach rooted in values of empathy, justice and service.

One seminal experience arrived unplanned during undergraduate study abroad in Southeast Asia. Living alone immersed in poverty-stricken villages awakened perspectives through surrounding realities far removed from privileged upbringing. Witnessing rampant disease, lack of basic resources and oppression's stranglehold from within that system jolted preconceptions.

Disillusionment mounted as attempts granting aid proved short-lived band aids upon deeply entrenched societal ills. Despair threatened abandoning the experience as a lost cause until stumbling upon grassroots organizers campaigning for systemic change from within.

Their model of fostering dignified empowerment through communal solidarity and nonviolent civil disobedience renewed hope despite immense obstacles. Realizing top-down solutions alone could never uplift populations, sustainable transformation required grassroots buy-in harnessing collective agency. This affirmed that true justice stems from inclusion, not charity or force, by addressing root realities not symptoms alone.

Witnessing their success cultivated through patience, wisdom and moral courage stirred leadership calling embracing strategic long-game reforms from ground up. This formative period cultivated a dedication to non-profit and political work confronting deep-seated challenges through community collaboration instead of saviorism

Several years later, transitioning into private sector leadership surfaced tensions between calling and navigating complex corporate dynamics. Early missteps occurred prioritizing perceived expectations over values through misguided people-pleasing.

But taking a stand for ethical conduct during an acquisition exposed unhealthy power dynamics threatening major losses. While controversial, refusing complicity-built trust with those impacted. After much soul-searching, a career shift pursued social ventures merging purpose and profits through innovative solutions.

There, leading diverse teams tackling systemic problems like lack of healthcare accessibility through passion strengthened resolve integrating values into strategy.

Leading with intention demanded navigating adversity, such as when one program faced widespread backlash.

Disillusionment arose considering alternative paths until remembering formative lessons. Recalling organizers' perseverance cultivation grassroots empowerment reframed challenges as temporary yet solvable through unity instead of division. Regrouping focused on addressing root concerns driving opposition through respectful dialogue where all voices felt heard and validated. While compromise arose, staying solution-oriented rebuilt trust transforming former opponents into allies committed to positive change.

Later in life, marriage and parenthood surfaced fresh priorities reshaping leadership motivations on societal level. Witnessing family navigate obstacles amplified resolve confronting injustices like lack of paid leave policies and unaffordable childcare disproportionately impacting women and lower income families.

Joining advocacy networks lobbying legislators strengthened value of service beyond immediate organization into upstream policy reform uplifting entire communities. And embracing parenting imperfections normalized vulnerability cultivating empathy for diverse struggles facing all.

While individual experiences uniquely influence each leader, certain common threads emerged fundamentally shaping my ongoing approach centered on empowerment and justice through inclusion.

From confronting disadvantages first-hand to overcoming adversity through unity instead of division, leadership lessons stem most potently from directly addressing root challenges of communities in contextualized manner. And a personal dedication arises motivating upstream reform cultivating systemic empowerment and dignity for all through approaches emphasizing cooperation over unilateralism.

A life devoted to walking alongside others navigating shared struggles nourishes empathy and purpose guiding lifelong service.

1.4 Authentically sharing career challenges and personal growth

Authentic leadership demands bringing our whole selves into the role through vulnerability and lived experiences. For me, openly sharing challenges illuminated ongoing growth and fostered meaningful connections.

However, initially discomfort loomed admitting weaknesses even to myself after decades conditioning success through image and bravado alone. Over time, small acts of courage paved the way to authentically sharing leadership lessons learned through failures alongside triumphs in ways empowering others.

A watershed moment occurred during a low point early in my corporate career, where micromanaging damaged team morale. Realizing mistakes demanded humility and rebuilding trust through transparency, a difficult admission addressed how power dynamics contributed to harm done.

While vulnerability stirred dread, opening up catalyzed reflective discussions restoring relationships. Witnessing painful truths acknowledged without defensiveness inspired new perspectives on psychologically safe cultures where people felt empowered addressing uncomfortable realities collaboratively.

Thereafter, sharing struggles became a leadership tool strengthening purpose beyond transactional roles alone.

From there, speaking engagements incorporated stories of career turbulence where values clashes arose. For example, facing an ultimatum to compromise ethics amid industry pressure illuminated tensions authentic leaders navigate daily.

Detailing thought processes around taking a principled stand countering unrealistic expectations modeled navigating ambiguity through resolve instead of people-pleasing alone. Similarly, divulging struggles leading through systemic racism exposed blind spots still plaguing progress and surfaced dialogues uniting diverse stakeholders toward reform. Authenticity proved disarming prejudice by establishing common ground of shared humanity beyond outward differences.

Along this progression, personal life lessons infiltrated professional contexts. For instance, candidly sharing about difficult divorce navigated with two young children facilitated discussions around prioritizing family amid demanding roles.

Normalizing emotional experiences lessened isolation facing parallel private turmoil. Expressing parenting imperfections fostered compassion amid colleagues' diverse responsibilities outside work. Bringing the total human experience, not just curated highlights, into work relationships built culture where everyone's humanity felt recognized versus compartmentalized.

While discomfort accompanied initial vulnerability, witnessing impacts inspired further candor. Revealing struggles facing paralysis of perfectionism encouraged experimenting beyond perceived limitations. Detailing mental health journeys pursuing treatment dismantled stigmas allowing people to bring full selves without fear of consequences.

Opening up about imposter syndrome surfacing in new arenas quelled doubts through supportive discussions confirming shared fallibility. Each authentic disclosure strengthen bonds of mutual understanding replacing illusion of solitary success with empowerment through interdependence.

Over a decade, courage to authentically share lived realities cemented as a leadership model emphasizing psychological safety and holistic well-being above performative positivity.

My personal growth emerged through these uncomfortable yet impactful dialogues where challenges illuminated collective humanity. Progress came not from climbing ladders alone but cultivating community.

While discomfort lingers disclosing imperfections, leadership purpose arises through authentic modeling so others feel empowered bringing multidimensional lives, not curated images, to workplaces as a means of driving transformational cultures maximizing humanity's potential through unity instead of division. Our shared vulnerabilities connect us beyond superficial differences, and authentic sharing cultivates justice by enfranchising all aspects of our experiences.

Chapter 02

Leading with Purpose and Values Alignment

Authentic leadership begins with understanding ourselves - our motivations, strengths, growth areas, and core values. However, true north also requires aligning our leadership approach with an inspiring purpose greater than any single role or achievement.

Only by anchoring our work in values does integrity and resilience emerge through challenges questioning direction. In Chapter 1, we explored my ongoing evolution developing self-awareness through intimate reflection and crucible experiences. This chapter shifts focus beyond inward excavation toward cultivating an authentic leadership approach staying principled amid complex realities through coherence.

Leading with an honorable purpose demands clarity separating personal values from imposed shoulds clouding intuition. For too long, I confused externally defined metrics of success like prestigious roles, salary increases and positive reviews for inner convictions guiding decisions.

Fulfilling others' expectations took priority over discerning motivations driving relentless performance. Misalignment surfaced through burnout, restlessness and moments questioning what truly mattered most. Transitioning from this autopilot required considerable self-evaluation to untangle intrinsic purpose from imposed standards of worth.

One tool facilitating values clarity involved visualizing approaching life's end while reviewing major decisions and relationships. Imagining these reflections illuminated which moments brought deepest fulfillment and regret. Through this exercise, themes emerged of cherishing connections empowering others through challenges instead of accolades alone.

Major life lessons involved walking alongside communities navigating adversity, where small acts of solidarity and justice disrupted cycles of disadvantage. Core values of empathy, integrity and service crystalized motivating continual growth outside comfort zones.

Of course, discerning purpose involved more than visualization - consistent application anchored each choice. For instance, early confusion surrounded career pivots where purpose shifted from profits alone toward social missions.

Questioning followed non-linear progression understanding core drives evolved contextually versus a fixed destination. However, consistency surfaced through recalibrating approaches like refusing to compromise ethics despite industry pressures. Or prioritizing family well-being amid organizational demands by establishing healthy boundaries.

Over time, decision-making coherence emerged from orienting internally instead of reactions chasing approval.
Applying values amid complexity posed ongoing challenges requiring perseverance and community support. For example, leading through systemic gender inequities amplified tensions between calling justice and navigating entrenched power dynamics.

Burnout threatened during exhaustive advocacy facing relentless micro and macro aggressions weakening resolve. Recharging involved trusted circles processing experiences without judgment while cultivating resilience through unity instead of isolation. Similarly, serving diverse constituencies necessitated navigating competing priorities through thoughtful discussion elevating shared values over manufactured division.

While coherence strengthened through practice, doubts surfaced periodically questioning motivations or direction.

During such moments, reflecting on lessons crystallizing purpose reassured continued evolvement versus arrival. For example, recalling pivotal experiences like witnessing grassroots organizers triumph against all odds renew commitment to empowering marginalized voices through patience and strategic partnership. Honoring mentors who walked similarly difficult roads supplying wisdom and accountability renewed energy. Ultimately, purpose emerged not as a fixed destination but an evolving North Star requiring continuous refinement amid life's perplexing terrain.

This chapter explores in-depth my ongoing journey aligning leadership approach with an evolving yet coherent internal compass centered on service, justice and empowerment.

Through stories of navigating complexity, growth and renewal of purpose, my hope is to offer a modeled process facilitating values clarity and coherence for any leader.

Authentic presence connects what we believe with how we show up daily through consistency even when easier paths beckon. By cultivating courage to stay anchored amid challenges, integrity and resilience emerge empowering sustainable progress far beyond any single achievement alone could provide. Our shared humanity calls us to lead honoring this perpetual journey.

2.1 Defining a higher purpose beyond external goals/metrics

While goals and metrics provide structure, reducing purpose solely to external benchmarks risks missing deeper motivations.

For years, my leadership purpose centered achievement through prestigious roles and applause measured by likes rather than why certain responsibilities mattered profoundly. However, aligning impact with deeper intrinsic drives requires disentangling purpose from imposed expectations through honest self-reflection on what uplifts humanity. For me, recalibrating focus involved examining assumptions, seeking clarity on principles animating lifelong service despite changing contexts, and cultivating renewed purpose through community.

Early confusion arose positioning aspirations within restrictive constructs of prestige and status. Success stemmed more from admiration than meaningful work benefiting others. However, introspection exposed deeper yens inspiring relentless effort typically dismissed as impractical "pipe dreams."

Recallings formative moments witnessing systemic oppression's toll amplified intrinsic motivation toward justice—not as lofty ideals but through strategic every day acts dismantling obstacles others faced. These recollections surfaced during low points when burnout tempted abandoning causes for stability alone.

To reconcile purpose discrepancy, reflective journaling dissected subconscious scripts still dictating self-worth. Discussions with confidantes facilitated separating narrative conditionings from core values like empathy, integrity and lifting marginalized voices.

Detailing visions of a just world revealed intentions rooted not in self-aggrandizement, but cultivating community where shared humanity triumphed over manufactured divisions. These authentic conversations affirmed passions aligned with bettering society versus fulfilment through roles alone.

Transitioning away from externally defined success markers took courage to dismantle perceptions of "realistic" paths. Soul-searching involved letting go attachment to stability, prestige or financial security establishing purpose beyond transactional achievements.

Focus shifted inward toward principles driving daily sacrifices, and outward to communities where meaningful impact arose from walking alongside struggles instead of saviorism. This redirection meant prioritizing societal uplift above role responsibilities alone through approaches emphasizing empowerment and sustainability over temporary solutions.

Recalibrating awoke purpose rooted in cultivating systems uplifting disadvantaged populations through dignity, unity and grassroots determination. Goals centered dismantling obstacles through patient coalition-building where diverse voices felt respected instead of top-down directives. Impact stemmed less from projects alone than nurturing collective agency and representation within structures too long preserving inequities.

Transformation meant reforming issues on macro and micro levels from ground up by addressing root challenges, not surface manifestations.

Renewed purpose emerged not as a fixed end-point but an evolving target through humility, learning from varied perspectives, and adapting approaches contextually.

Mistakes surfaced opportunities for growth rather than deficiency—lessons enhanced strategies collaborating on complex challenges requiring multifaceted coordination.

Burnout risk ebbed through replenishing energy from communities where together progress felt inspiring versus lonely crusades against perceived problems alone. And service upheld integrity focusing outward to historically marginalized populations instead of chasing empty validation.

Of course, aligning purpose amid changing realities posed ongoing work anchoring motivations securely versus wavering reactions. For example, leadership roles emerged privileging technical skills over societal priorities tested resolve.
However, consistency arose compromising less and advocating more through respect, empathy and strategic partnership. Similarly, competing duties pulled attention from activism during parental responsibilities yet consistency surfaced prioritizing family well-being and reform benefiting future generations.

Cultivating a higher purpose anchored in justice, empowerment and sustaining progress emerged through community, reflection separating narratives from core motives, and recalibrating focus outward on collaboratively shaping equitable systems versus singular achievements alone.

Coherence strengthened persistently aligning daily actions with evolving principles of service despite complexity pushing temporary concessions. Authentic leadership arises from relationships where shared humanity feels respected over artificial obstacles and intrinsic drives uplift communities beyond superficial goals alone.

2.2 Translating Values into a Vision and Strategic Direction

Understanding core principles is merely the foundation - authentic leadership involves translating values into a coherent vision clearly communicated and operationalized through strategic planning. For years, lack of coherence hampered my efforts as purpose drifted between altruistic aims and ambitions dictated by situations instead of integrity.

Reform demanded aligning rhetoric with actions systematically moving society toward justice through achievable milestones versus amorphous dreams.

This transition first required unpacking assumptions still dictating priorities versus principles. Breaking down preconceived strategies through diverse lenses exposed unintentional biases compromising vision.

For example, tendency arose helping those resembling my background avoiding discomfort challenging safe spaces. Excavating such residual conditionings took humility yet strengthened commitments aligning activities holistically.

Similarly, assessing burnout risks revealed unsustainable pace driven by need for external validation instead of purpose.

Values clarity prompted reimagining work comprehensively coordinating efforts across silos through strategic synergies. Recalibrating involved delineating step-by-step pathways toward envisioned world sustained beyond singular roles.

Concrete plans connected short, medium and long-term aims coordinated pragmatically through various stages. For example, certain objectives centered dismantling disadvantages through representation, partnering grassroots leaders amplifying unheard voices instead of directives.

Mid-range goals involved systemic reforms cultivating equity through policies uplifting populations historically excluded from decision-making.

Coalition-building emerged as a key strategic direction aligning diverse stakeholders toward shared higher purpose yet allowing flexibility navigating uncertainty. For example, convening advocacy networks unified various missions facilitating holistic progress beyond any solo agenda. Similarly, uniting professionals across industries nurtured coordinated campaigns tackling interconnected challenges like poverty through multifaceted approaches. And empowering communities centralized local visions aggregating grassroots determination into upstream reforms made accessible through education instead of reaction.

Regular reevaluation maintained strategic agility adapting promptly to changing landscapes through learning versus rigidity. For instance, redirecting resources emerged during crises where underserved populations suffered disproportionate impacts.

However, consistency arose reorienting quick toward economic recovery through equitable structures versus temporary relief alone.

Overall, authentic leadership efficacy surfaced not from perfect planning but aligning daily activities systematically through community toward a just world where shared humanity triumphs through empowerment and reciprocity instead of manufactured conflict. While values clarity lays the groundwork, authentic coherence also requires clearly communicating vision and strategic direction.

Early in my leadership journey, inconsistency arose between ambitions and rhetoric fueling doubt and stagnation. Reform involved intentionally operationalizing purpose through transparent conversations bringing broader perspectives into strategic planning.

One approach centered uniting diverse stakeholders in crafting long term objectives ensuring plans encompassed varied realities. For example, convening discussions across generations surfaced perspective gaps where strategies addressed surface issues instead of root barriers dismantling opportunities for youth.

Similarly, partnering professionals from various life stages and backgrounds highlighted unintentional biases overlooking obstacles some populations disproportionately faced. These insight exchanges strengthened commitments aligning vision holistically.

Accessibility also became paramount relaying comprehensive yet digestible visions leveraging varied mediums. Concise messaging unified communications coordinating efforts across silos.

For example, disseminating short mission statements and quarterly milestones through accessible platforms like newsletters and social media streams clearly outlined how daily responsibilities connected to holistic strategies.

Livestreamed roundtables and Q&As brought further transparency discussing challenges, revisions and successes without pretense.

Consistency emerged integrating purpose across personal and professional spheres. For instance, candidly discussing activism and volunteer work at industry events bridged purpose between work responsibilities and intrinsic motivations.

Webinars incorporating family anecdotes modeling integrity navigating life's complexity strengthened relatability. And using platforms like podcast interviews to share mistakes and critiques countering echo chambers fostered humility motivating continual growth.

Of course, purpose coherence posed daily challenges keeping ambitions in sync amid uncertainty through unity instead of reaction. For example, unexpected crises tested transparency approaching issues strategically from ground up through empathy and learning versus directives.

Committing to recalibrating solutions collaboratively maintained vision alignment.

Overall, authentic leadership sustainability required ongoing work clearly yet accessibly communicating strategic direction holistically through relationships instead of top-down proclamations alone. Together, purpose thrives beyond personas by nurturing empowerment through shared determinations.

2.3 Making values-based decisions through transparency

Authentic leadership depends not just on defining coherent purpose and direction, but consistently enacting values even when risky. For too long, I wavered compromising integrity for shallow gains like appeasing critics or chasing superficial metrics.

However, staying true necessitates navigating complexity transparently guided by intrinsic north stars versus reactions alone. This tested me repeatedly to make courageous choices uplifting humanity through respectful discourse over quick fixes or unilateralism.

Early challenges arose standing against normalized corruption threatening harms. For example, opposing legislative maneuvers legalizing predatory practices demanded rigorous discussions elevating marginalized voices silenced by manufactured consent campaigns.

Progress meant reframing issues systematically through empathy exposing root causes fueling problems instead of scapegoating alone. Transparency emerged dismantling harmful narratives piece by piece through data where all could evaluate rationally.

Of course, taking principled stands stirred tension necessitating wisdom navigating opposition diplomatically. Comingling personal ambitions risked backlash undermining broader missions. However, consistency arose committing dialogue over division through patience, appeals to shared values and collaborative solutions wherever feasible. Accepting some views required time amid ingrained assumptions showed humility motivating reconsiderations versus accusations escalating polarization.

And acknowledging imperfect understanding of others' perspectives fostered cooperation over conflict addressing intertwined root causes.

Leading innovation through disruption posed parallel tests balancing risk and responsibility. Transformations demanded navigating risk-aversion inhibiting growth through cautious experimentation. However, reckless changes could harm communities if missing mark. Striking this balance took thoughtful piloting scaled purposefully involving stakeholders coordinating learning through changes neither too slow stagnating progress nor swift threatening stability.

For example, certain initiatives benefited disenfranchised groups through accessible technologies if navigating digital divides sensitively from lived expertise.

Complex tradeoffs arose around allocating limited resources where perfect answers proved elusive. However, transparency emerged channeling funds holistically through inclusive prioritization discussions incorporating community needs assessment.

For instance, certain investments centered developing community leaders' capacity building skills through accessible educational programs. And collaboration emphasized long-term sustainability empowering disadvantaged populations toward self-sufficiency over temporary fixes alone.

Navigating crises tested consistency thoroughly through ambiguous problems requiring speed yet thoughtfulness.

Quickly addressing disproportionate impacts on marginalized communities took prioritizing resources holistically through grassroots partnerships instead of unilateral directives.

However, redirecting focus toward recovery through just systems meant diligently assessing consequences to avoid worsening preexisting disadvantages. Calmly discussing alternate views strengthened cooperative solutions uplifting humanity through shared determination.

Of course, authenticity posed daily challenges amid complexity where integrity occasionally felt simpler than solving problems respectfully. However, consistency emerged through candor inviting critical feedback, appeals to shared convictions guiding choices, and recalibrating transparently through community.

While risks accompanied standing for justice and human dignity, authentic coherence strengthened societies navigating struggles together compassionately instead of reactively alone. Our shared humanity calls leaders to enact values inclusively through candor where people feel empowered addressing realities cooperatively.

Consistency takes dedicated work maintaining integrity amid divergent views, whether from critics outwardly opposing stances or allies proposing alternate paths forward. During such challenges, anchoring choices in shared principles while welcoming transparency strengthens coherence.

For instance, opposing legislation emerged through thorough discussion of root issues fueling harms instead of reaction. Respectfully addressing dissent involved dissecting objections point-by-point through an equity lens focused on proportional and least restrictive solutions. Calmly acknowledging merits amid critique invited further partnership where possible navigating nuances collaboratively instead of division. Consistency arose seeking common ground of justice and human dignity through patience whenever feasible.

Similarly, aligning diverse allies toward coherent strategies continually engaged varying perspectives through transparency. Regular discussions incorporated learning across silos bringing wisdom yet unseen vantage points into recalibrating approaches contextually. For example, roundtable conversations elevated concerns where certain plans unintentionally risked exacerbating preexisting burdens on some communities. Listening without defensiveness and recalibrating holistically maintained integrity.

Of course, complexity arose where perfect consensus proved elusive yet timely action imperative. During such debates, anchoring choices in shared convictions of empowerment and equity strengthened coherence. For instance, certain investments held potential helping underserved groups access opportunities if carefully piloted from ground up.

Consistency emerged cautiously testing changes sensitively through learning instead of reactions while meaningfully assessing unintentional impacts.

Overall, authentic decision-making emerged through candor inviting multiple vantage points rationally discussing alternatives focused on justice and dignity for all. Humility strengthened integrity acknowledging imperfect information requiring ongoing growth.

And transparency built trust navigating dilemmas collaboratively toward progress instead of unilateralism alone.

Consistency upheld values even amid dissent through appeals to shared convictions of unity, equity and mutual understanding whenever possible over division. Our shared humanity calls leaders to enact purpose inclusively and with care for one another.

2.4 Inspiring commitment through consistency of words and actions

Authentic leadership hinges on aligning rhetoric with integrity demonstrated through day-to-day decisions. For too long, I wavered between grand ambitions and compromising purpose to appease critics or pursue superficial gains alone. However, inspiring commitment necessitates consistency guiding communities navigating struggles together through resilience instead of rigid directives.

This tested me to enact values boldly yet respectfully through candor where rhetoric matched reality demonstrating humankind's potential through cooperation over division.

Early challenges arose reforming corrupted systems upholding inequities through normalized apathy and detachment. Inspiring activism required dismantling harmful narratives strategically by reframing issues from lived experiences fueling problems instead of reactionary stances alone. For example, convenings provided space for marginalized voices historically excluded from debates to redefine challenges facing communities and propose community-centered solutions through empathy and data.

Consistency emerged committing funds and efforts to seeding equitable solutions piloted sensitively from ground up. Pilot programs focused on cultivating local leadership and self-sufficiency through accessible skills and networks reducing dependency on temporary fixes alone.

Similarly, advocacy unified stakeholders coordinating efforts dismantling obstacles confronted jointly respecting humanity across perceived differences. Progress meant reforming systems from within through grassroots representation instead of reactionary directives alone. Of course, navigating opposition demanded consistency navigating dissent with care, wisdom and strategic appeals to shared principles.

Comingling personal stances risked distracting from greater justice missions, yet silence condoned inaction. Solutions centered bringing parties together to advance shared interests through understanding instead of conflict alone.

Accepting imperfect information, I acknowledged each perspective with empathy and commitment discussing alternatives focusing on equitable, least restrictive paths forward through cooperation over ultimatums. Consistency strengthened societies compassionately navigating struggles collectively instead of reactionary commands alone.

For example, certain initiatives invested in accessible technologies if empowering historically disadvantaged groups through digital skills and oversight ensuring tools uplifted communities sensitively.

Progress balanced risk and responsibility through pilot programs scaled purposefully involving stakeholders coordinating sustainable innovations addressing root causes jointly. Overall, consistency emerged guiding cooperation over unilateralism through appeals to our shared humanity.

Consistency took courage amid complexity where integrity sometimes felt simpler than thoughtfully solving problems together. However, anchoring choices in mutual understanding and equity through transparency built trust navigating dilemmas. For example, crises demanded balancing urgent action with assessing unintended impacts carefully through grassroots partnership. And aligning diverse missions demanded regular discussion elevating marginalized voices and recalibrating holistically to strengthen, not weaken shared convictions.

Inspiring commitment emerged through consistency matching ambitious rhetoric with integrity demonstrated daily through transparent decisions elevating shared interests over superficial divisions.

Humility acknowledged imperfect information requiring patience and care navigating discord jointly instead of directives alone. And consistency upholding justice and human dignity through appeals to our higher nature strengthened progressive movements sustainable beyond personas by nurturing cooperation through unity in our shared humanity.

While integrity builds trust long-term, consistency also strengthens retention amid daily complexities potentially compromising coherence. During such challenges, anchoring choices in shared values through transparency and community support nourishes commitment.

For example, opposing legislation involved respectfully addressing dissent by thoughtfully discussing objections and alternative solutions focused on justice and least harm.

Consistency emerged seeking understanding and cooperation over reaction through patience and invitation wherever possible navigating nuances collaboratively instead of division. Similarly, aligning diverse stakeholders toward coherent strategies engaged varying viewpoints to strengthen strategies contextually instead of unilateralism.

Consistency took humility adapting approaches where unintended oversights emerged disproportionately impacting some communities. For instance, certain initiatives aimed empowering underserved groups through digital equity if overseen sensitively and recalibrated promptly incorporating learning. Progress balanced timely action with carefully assessing unforeseen impacts through grassroots partnership.

Anchoring integrity amid disagreement and learning strengthened consistency even when swifter options seemed simpler. For example, crises demanded prioritizing urgent response yet carefully considering consequences to vulnerable populations holistically.

Transparency emerged recalibrating approaches cooperatively instead of directives alone by inviting multifaceted expertise into discussions. Committing resources required navigating tradeoffs strategically through inclusive prioritization and pilot programs involving stakeholders.

Aligning rhetoric with integrity in decision-making nourished trust and commitment by consistently upholding principles of empathy, cooperation and care for humanity through candor. Humility strengthened consistency acknowledging imperfect understanding requiring community wisdom navigating complexities jointly toward justice and dignity for all through appeals to our shared convictions instead of reaction alone. Our humanity calls leaders to lead with these values of unity and care through transparent integrity.

***

Chapter 03

Building Trust Through Vulnerability

Authentic leadership arises from aligning values with integrity through consistency even amid complexity. However, demonstrating coherence poses daily challenges requiring courage navigating uncertainty with care, wisdom and transparency.

For many years, I wavered between grand ambitions and temporarily compromising purpose to appease shifting perceptions or chase fleeting gains alone.

However, cultivating communities sustained through resilience demands modeling vulnerability through candor where rhetoric matches reality demonstrating humankind's potential through cooperation instead of division or directives. This tested me repeatedly to stay guided by principles of justice, empathy and mutual understanding through humility.

Early in my leadership journey, inconsistency emerged between lofty aims and compromising purpose reactively through people-pleasing alone. Internal pressures still conditioned self-worth through external approval instead of inner purpose. However, empowering diversity within movements necessitates recognizing our shared fallibilities through relationships built upon candor, not just competence.

Transitioning required dismantling hidden scripts of perfectionism through thoughtful reflection on formative experiences, fears and yearnings driving service which society too often marginalizes as weaknesses.

Sharing such perceived deficiencies with care and intention initially felt terrifying possibly exposing raw spots to exploitation. However, risks accompanied maintaining façades disconnecting rhetoric from humanity potentially undermining integrity long-term.

Transitioning involved reimagining vulnerability as relationship-building rather than deficiency through transparent discussions dismantling stigmas attached to discussing mental health, imperfection and personal growth without defensiveness or pretense.

Progress centered cultivating cultures where people felt empowered bringing full, multidimensional experiences versus curated highlights into spaces without fear of consequences.

Of course, practicing vulnerability demanded perseverance amid pressures still conditioning worth through performance alone. For example, acknowledging burnout risks and limitations surfaced needs for replenishment yet initially stirred self-doubt exposing inadequacies. However, sharing struggles with care and seeking support demonstrated fallibility as universal versus personal faults.

Discussing challenges from places of learning cultivated understanding of humanity's shared capacity for growth through interdependence overcoming division.

Leadership lessons emerged not from arriving flawlessly but navigating imperfections with courage, care, transparency and community.

For example, certain pilot programs faced tensions requiring recalibration conversations acknowledging stumbles strengthened strategies instead of condemnation. And acknowledging missteps upfront while appealing to shared purpose invited collaborative problem-solving reflecting light instead of shadows.

Vulnerability emerged as relationship-building rather than deficiency through appeals to our interdependent humanity.

This chapter explores my ongoing evolution cultivating trustworthiness through transparency about life's inherent struggles navigated with wisdom, care and community.

By modeling acknowledgement of limitations and ongoing growth with humility, my hope is to contribute to transforming perceived vulnerabilities from areas of fear into strengths through relationships where people feel empowered bringing multidimensional experiences and shared humanity into spaces.

When authenticity connects what we profess with imperfect yet courageous modeling, integrity and resilience emerge empowering progress through cooperation instead of conflict alone. Our shared experiences call us to lead and walk alongside one another with candor, care, empathy and hope.

3.1 Understanding how vulnerability builds credibility

For too long, perceived strength centered image maintenance through performance alone instead of integrity navigated fallibly yet empathetically. However, cultivating trust requires modeling humanity's shared capacity through transparency about limitations and growth amid complex realities.

Credibility emerges by authentically connecting rhetoric with lived experiences demonstrating care, wisdom and community whenever progress feels uncertain.

Early attempts bringing full experiences felt terrifying exposing raw spots vulnerable to exploitation or judgment. Internalized pressures conditioned worth through eloquence and expertise alone instead of shared imperfection.

Transitioning involved unpacking assumptions through reflective discussions dismantling notions vulnerability equated weakness versus humanity. For example, acknowledging burnout risks and needs for replenishment strengthened commitments to restoring balance through support systems instead of soldiering on reactively.

Practice emerged through candidly sharing formative struggles where formative missteps taught precious lessons cultivating resilience and empathy.

Detailing career pivots navigating values clashes and adapting purpose contextually normalized nonlinear progression embracing learning from mistakes non-defensively. Similarly, openly discussing personal hardships like divorce navigated compassionately strengthened relatability beyond curated highlights alone. Vulnerability surfaced as relationship-building demonstrating shared capacity for growth through stumbles resolved with community.

Leading change amid complexity meant modeling limitations openly yet with hope. For example, acknowledging tensions where certain initiatives faced learning curves invited collaboratively problem-solving light instead of shadows through appeals to shared purpose.

Similarly, discussing challenges orchestrating responses proportionately through crises without premeditated formulas embraced learning from varied expertise uniting shared humanity. Credibility arose navigating uncertainties together versus reactions alone.

Consistency emerged authentically connecting strengths with areas still developing without pretense or defensiveness. For instance, certain discussions brought full yet imperfect experiences navigating systemic oppression and advocating justice with care, wisdom and recognition of biases still evolving.

Progress centered cultivating safe spaces encouraging others similarly sharing stumbles resolved through interdependence instead of isolation.

Our shared humanity emerged stronger through such dialogues emphasizing rehabilitation over recrimination.

Vulnerability proved disarming, not debilitating by demonstrating shared fallibility as relatable versus reproach. By modeling ongoing evolution sincerely yet constructively, consistency empowered broader unity navigating struggles collectively.

Credibility was evident through transparency authentically matching rhetoric with lived experiences navigating complexities with care, empathy and appeals to our shared capacity for growth and resilience and mutual support. When authenticity connects what we profess with imperfect yet courageous living guided by justice, integrity and hope, progress thrives through cooperation instead of conflict alone.

While bringing fuller experiences strengthens relationships, vulnerability also poses risks requiring care, wisdom and community. For example, exposing perceived weaknesses potentially invites exploitation or devaluation instead of understanding.

Transitioning involved cultivating spaces empowering openness through empathy, not judgment.

Discussing struggles centered learning versus recrimination by appealing to humanity's shared capacity for growth through interdependence. Progress emerged normalizing discussions of limitations, barriers and ongoing evolution without stigma through supportive dialogue.

Consistency surfaced in mentoring others similarly navigating complexities with compassion. For instance, sharing hardships like burnout and parenting amid obligations normalized struggles as universal rather than personal failure.

Guiding vulnerable conversations modeled resolving tensions constructively by appealing to purpose and shared resilience within community.

Choosing candor deliberately strengthened plausibility versus compulsion. Timing acknowledged contexts where certain disclosures risked distracting from justice missions ormanipulation. However, consistency emerged prioritizing integrity through wisdom navigating uncertainty together versus alone.

Humility recognized imperfect leading requiring continual learning even when easier paths felt simpler.

For example, certain initiatives faced tensions requiring recalibrationthrough collaborative problem-solving instead of deflection. And acknowledging misstepsconstructively invited cooperative growthreflecting light from varied perspectives uniting shared humanity.

Integrity appeared authentically connecting strengths with ongoing development through transparency, empathy and appeals to our interdependence. When authenticity matches words with respectful modeling guided by justice, care and hope, integrity empowers confronting challenges collectively instead of reactively alone.

3.2 Sharing failures and lessons learned with humility

For too long, vulnerabilities felt threatening possibly undermining perceived strength through image alone. However, cultivating trust requires authentically connecting rhetoric with humanity's shared experiences navigating uncertainties through interdependence versus isolation.

By sharing failures and ongoing growth sincerely yet constructively with humility and care for community, progress emerges through cooperation instead of division.

Early attempts sharing failures felt terrifying laying bare imperfections potentially exploited as weaknesses versus opportunities.

Formative missteps felt shameful reflecting solely on perceived faults instead of universal lessons strengthening shared resilience. However, practices evolved recognizing humanity's capacity through transparency about limitations courageously overcome through wisdom and support systems.

Consistency emerged thoughtfully detailing risks accompanying innovation boldly pursued yet imperfectly realized through humble acknowledgment requiring recalibration.

For example, certain pilot programs faced tensions teaching humility to recalibrate strategically by inviting collaborative problem-solving focusing on joint purpose.

Admitting miscalculations constructed light by emphasizing learning strengthens integrity over defensiveness. Similarly, discussing hardships growing into purpose through nonlinearity and pivots embraced shared imperfection.

Career crossroads navigated with care, empathy and community strengthened meaningful work aligning daily actions with evolving principles of justice through humility.

Progress centered cultivating understanding versus condemnation of humanity's shared experiences overcoming obstacles together instead of alone.

Leadership emerged through constructive vulnerability acknowledging areas still developing despite expertise in others. For instance, certain discussions brought full yet imperfect advocacy journeys navigating systemic oppression and championing justice with care, wisdom and recognition of biases still evolving.

Consistency involved mentoring others facing tensions by appealing to resilience within trusted relationships.

Humility proved empowering through transparency about limitations overcome cooperatively instead of reactions alone.

By sincerely sharing stumbles resolved constructively, consistency strengthens integrity inspiring collective efforts facing struggles together versus performative directives alone.

Together, our imperfect yet courageous experiences demonstrate humanity's shared capacity building trust through empathy, interdependence and hope.

While vulnerability takes courage, consistently practicing discernment strengthens trustworthiness. Early efforts lacked nuance potentially misunderstood carelessly shared. However, maturity emerged recognizing impacts of transparency through humility, empathy and care for community.

Consistency involved choreographing candor deliberately through reflection on contexts, timing and impacts on relationships. For example, certain exposures risked manipulation or distraction from purpose necessitating wisdom navigating receptiveness and repercussions carefully.

Intent centered strengthening integrity through appeals to justice, interdependence and growth instead of self-aggrandizement alone.

Humility acknowledged fallibility demanding diligence navigating ambiguity thoughtfully.

Not every venture proved just, nor option foreseeable requiring adaptability embracing complexity. Yet consistency arose owning mistakes courageously through appeals to shared learning focusing reconstruction over defense.

For instance, missteps fueled by ignorance instead of malice invited understanding navigating realities incompletely.

Admitting biases still clouding perspective strengthened commitment confronting blindspots cooperatively through open dialogue. Our imperfect journeys gaining awareness cultivate hope confronting struggles together versus alone.

Maturity emerged choreographing candor deliberately invoking empathy instead of condemnation. For example, failures disproportionately harming communities warranted humility repairing harms before disclosure or deflection.

And discussing tensions privately reinforced care, avoiding public shame strengthening restoration.
Consistency meant modeling receptiveness integrating critiques constructively.

While concerns felt inconvenient, integrity emerged addressing valid criticisms calmly and correcting course jointly instead of reactions. Our shared experiences navigating uncertainties strengthens movements embracing imperfections resolved constructively.

Humility proved empowering through sincerity addressing struggles holistically with community.
When authenticity matches words with respectful living guided by justice, care and appeal to humanity's shared capacity for growth, trust emerges empowering cooperation confronting complexities collectively.
Together, we can cultivate understanding that setbacks arise not from personal flaws, but navigation of realities imperfectly yet courageously resolved through wisdom and fellowship.

3.3 Active listening and connecting beyond surface level

Vulnerability proves empowering through understanding our shared experiences navigating life's ambiguities imperfectly yet diligently with community.

However, meaningful connection demands attentiveness embracing multidimensionality beyond cursory interactions alone. For too long, performative strengths undermined integrity disconnecting rhetoric from humanity.

Transitioning called reflecting on motivations prioritizing performance over presence which distance relationships. Interactions felt curated fulfilling perceived obligations instead of candid fellowship cultivating shared welfare.

Formative influences conditioned worth through superficial validation alone neglecting depth strengthening society.

Consistency emerged recognizing each experience, though varied, nurtures humanity equally. Prior commitments focused narrow self-interests disconnected communities facing struggles jointly.

Transition involved cultivating presence through reflective listening dismantling hidden scripts privileging expertise over empathy. Maturity emerged nurturing understanding from places of learning, not proving alone.

Practice surfaced dismantling barriers through respectful engagement across perceived differences.

Preconceptions risked imposing narratives absent lived wisdoms instead of gleaning perspectives openly. Progress centered inviting full contributions without judgement through attentiveness embracing divergences strengthening diversity.

Active listening dismantled obstacles through patience and care for shared growth. Presumptions clouded receptiveness necessitating discernment embracing complexity versus reactivity.

Consistency emerged navigating struggles together from ground up appreciating humanity in all its beauty through cooperation instead of directives alone.

Interactions felt deeper acknowledging no experience carried more weight, though outwardly varied.

Stories nurtured fellowship recognizing life's shared joys and hardships beyond superficial comparisons. Together, we cultivated understanding that experiences teach lessons beyond perceived merits alone.

Attentiveness strengthened integrity beyond self through presence embracing opportunities as blessings, not obligations.

Consistency recognized each contribution, though different, affirmed our shared capacity for wisdom, goodness and justice navigating uncertainties imperfectly yet courageously as one.

Certain disclosures faced prejudice necessitating discernment embracing complexities beyond initial reactions.

Progress centered inviting full contributions without prejudice through attentiveness, not cursory engagement alone.

Nuanced perspectives arose dismantling obstacles through patience, care and recognition of humanity in all its beauty. Similarly, active listening strengthened community navigating struggles jointly from grassroots instead of directives alone.

Interactions felt deeper acknowledging no experience carried inherently more significance, though outwardly differing. Stories nurtured fellowship recognizing life's shared joys and hardships beyond superficial comparisons alone.

Consistency involved recognizing each contribution, though distinct, affirmed our shared capacity for wisdom, growth, justice and care navigating uncertainties imperfectly yet courageously as one people.

Attentiveness focused collective welfare over isolated agenda strengthening integrity beyond self through presence and candor.

Maturity emerged cultivating spaces where people felt empowered bringing layered realities vulnerably without fear of exploitation or reductionism.

Safe dialogues dismantled barriers through empathy recognizing experiences teach lessons beyond outward merits alone. Transformation centered inviting fullness through respect instead of cursory engagement or assumptions.

Progress embraced complexity navigating ambiguities jointly from ground up through appeals to our shared humanity. Active listening prioritized attentiveness over expertise strengthening fellowship by dissolving obstacles and affirming diverse yet equally meaningful contributions united us.

Consistency arose dismantling hidden scripts privileging some voices through humility and care for community.

Together, we cultivated understanding experiences teach varied yet equally invaluable wisdoms navigating life's shared beauty and struggles as one. When authentic presence connects rhetoric with sincerely embracing multiplicity, integrity emerges empowering cooperation confronting uncertainties collectively instead of reactions alone.

Our humanity calls all people to engage and walk alongside one another with candor, empathy and hope.

3.4 Resolving conflicts through empathetic dialogue

Building trust through vulnerability necessitates embracing complexity constructively. However, tensions inevitably arise despite shared purpose requiring wisdom navigating differences respectfully.

For too long, reactions risked escalating conflicts instead of resolution through understanding. Transitioning demanded cultivating spaces where dissent felt safe dismantling obstacles through cooperation, not division alone.

Early leadership deemed disagreement threatening potentially undermining authority through compliance alone.

However, integrity emerges navigating ambiguities together from places of learning, not control. Resolving tensions authentically involves cultivating empathetic dialogues where all parties feel heard and validated through candor without fear of reprisal.

Consistency surfaced recognizing opposing stances as equally informed though differing, not antagonistic perspectives warranting consideration, not deflection.

Progress centered appeals to shared values of justice, dignity and care for community over unilateral directives potentially deepening divides.

Our humanity calls for navigating struggles collectively from ground up through empathy instead of reactions alone.

Transitioning called cultivating safe dialogues dismantling barriers by embracing divergent views respectfully and addressing underlying interests cooperatively.

Presumptions risked imposing narratives detached from realities worsening conflicts instead of reconciliation. Maturity emerged navigating differences patiently from places of learning together versus alone through cooperation and fellowship.

Vulnerability proved empowering through transparency recognizing imperfect information necessitating joint navigation of uncertainties.

Discussions focused understanding motivations driving positions thoughtfully without prejudice strengthening empathy over preconceptions potentially intensifying discord.

Consistency emerged steering resolutions prioritizing shared purpose of dignity for all through appeals to humanity's capacity for growth within community.

Integrity began navigating tensions respectfully from grassroots through appeals to our interdependence, not compliance alone. When authentic relationships connect rhetoric with sincerely embracing complexity, cooperation triumphs confronting uncertainties collectively instead of through reaction.

Our shared experiences call us to cultivate understanding through fellowship instead of division.
While disagreements arise naturally, transitions demanded cultivating spaces where dissent felt safe navigating differences constructively instead of defensively alone.

Formative experiences conditioned views threatening dissent as disloyalty necessitating corrective action instead of cooperative resolutions.

Consistency surfaced transitioning to integrity emerging from empowering respectful engagement across divergences strengthening diversity versus compliance alone.

Presumptions risked imposed narratives detached from realities potentially intensifying divides needlessly.

Maturity emerged recognizing imperfect information requiring joint navigation of uncertainties from places of shared growth.

For example, certain disclosures faced instinctive reactions necessitating patience and care dismantling preconceptions through open dialogue from places of learning together.

Progress centered appeals to justice, dignity and fellowship over unilateralism potentially exacerbating tensions through directives alone.

Shared purpose united addressing motivations driving positions thoughtfully without prejudice.

Vulnerability proved empowering through transparency navigating struggles collectively instead of emotionally alone.

Discussions focused cooperative problem-solving recognizing valid concerns strengthening empathy and welfare over individual agendas potentially intensifying discord.

Consistency emerged prioritizing shared humanity, not temporary victories exacerbating divides, through appeals to our interdependence and capacity for understanding within community.

Together, integrity emerged cultivating spaces where dissent felt respected and resolutions focused reconstructive diplomacy over damage control through humility and care.

When authentic relationships connect rhetoric with sincerely embracing complexity together, cooperation triumphs confronting imperfect information collectively instead of reactions exacerbating conflict alone. Our shared experiences call all people to resolve differences compassionately through willingness to understand one another.

While disagreements inevitably arise, wisdom emerges navigating divergences constructively through relationship-building instead of unilateral directives. Formative experiences conditioned conflict avoidance disconnecting rhetoric from realities necessitating transition.

Maturity involved cultivating spaces where dissent felt understood dismantling silos empowering respect across perceived "others". Progress centered appealing to our shared experiences imperfectly navigating life's struggles jointly instead of isolated preconceptions.

For example, acknowledging blindspots where ingrained biases clouded objective analysis invited cooperative exploration strengthening accountability. Similarly, discussions focusing underlying interests addressed motivations driving positions recognized struggles of diverse communities historically marginalized.

Together we dismantled barriers recognizing experiences unequally impacting humanity empowered jointly resolving tensions.

Consistency meant embracing imperfect information from places of learning, not proving alone.

Receptiveness to critiques, though inconvenient, meant addressing valid concerns and correcting course constructively. Shared fellowship emerged navigating uncertainties alongside one another compassionately through humility.

Framework shifted from compliance to empowering dignified engagement across differences.

Dissent felt respected through appeals to our capacity for growth within community instead of directives alone.

Resolutions focused reconstructive diplomacy recognizing no perspective inherently superior, though outwardly differing.

Together, authentic relationships dissolved obstacles by embracing complexity sincerely.

Understanding emerged from fellowship instead of isolated preconceptions. When rhetoric matched living as one, cooperation triumphed confronting ambiguities collectively as equally informed yet divergent partners in justice. Our humanity calls this approach of resolving differences through empathy and relationship-building.

***

Chapter 04

Inspiring Others Through Authentic Connection

While navigating change and maintaining integrity prove demanding on their own, true leadership emerges through empowering purpose beyond any single vision or tenure. Sustaining impact necessitates inspiring others according to their shared skills and humanity above fleeting directives potentially missing nuances of lived realities.

Wisdom surfaces cultivating spaces where communities feel heard, respected and mobilized through purpose connecting actions to values.

Leadership lessons gleaned emphasize authentic connection over isolated directives alone. Formative experiences risked detachment through image management prioritizing perceptions above structural reforms ensuring liberation proposed empowered dignity envisioned cooperatively from grassroots.

Transitioning demanded recognizing imperfect yet sincere progress surfaces through relationship-building navigating tradeoffs thoughtfully alongside one another.

Consistency emerged dismantling silos through appeals to fellowship across perceived differences in service of shared purpose. Early resistance fixated on directives risked weakening networks anchoring visions in realities navigated jointly instead of unilateral commands potentially missing diversity of invaluable wisdoms.

Progress centered cultivating forums where grassroots felt heard and inspired according to lives navigating inequalities thoughtfully.

This chapter explores inspiring positive change through genuine human connection empowering people according to skills and visions for justice traversed cooperatively. Authentic interaction fortifies integrity guiding words aligning with shared humanity experienced together navigating society's obstacles sincerely as respected partners confronting adversities collectively from within.

Wisdom recognizes each person's imperfect yet invaluable gifts for transforming realities navigated from places of care, empathy and fellowship.

Formative experiences risked detachment through image alone versus relationship-building across perceived divides.

Transitioning demands dismantling such barriers through consistent care, accountability and wisdom guiding appeal to our shared capacity for understanding navigating complexities compassionately as one dignified family above all else. Leadership emerges empowering purpose beyond positions through empowering grassroots networks as equally valued companions on the challenging road ahead.

For too long, detachment between rhetoric and realities privileged directives potentially missing diversity of lived wisdoms strengthened liberation visions through empowerment from ground up. Wisdom surfaced transitioning focus towards cultivating spaces where grassroots felt mobilized, not controlled alone according organizing skills and visions for shared humanity.

Progress centered appeals to fellowship over isolated agendas potentially fracturing ownership of transforming actualized envisioned cooperately.
Consistency involved cultivating environments where people experienced humanity's shared struggles and capacity for resilience through authentic care, accountability and empowerment of all lives' inherent worth above fleeting attributes dividing alone.

Formative experiences risked detachment through directives over relationship-building navigating uncertainties courageously together from grassroots. Transitioning dismantled such silos through empowering diversity of voices united in shared experience confronting society's obstacles collectively as one dignified family.

4.1 Motivating teams through care, compassion, appreciation

While inspiring positive change proves profoundly challenging, authentic leadership emerges empowering purpose through nurturing human connection across perceived divides. Sustaining impact necessitates cultivating environments where communities feel heard, respected and mobilized according to shared humanity experienced together navigating life's obstacles sincerely as valued companions.

Formative experiences risked detachment through directives prioritizing perceptions above relationship-building navigating tradeoffs thoughtfully alongside one another. Transitioning demands consistency fortifying integrity through appeals to fellowship empowering shared experiences above fleeting attributes dividing alone. Wisdom recognizes each person's imperfect yet invaluable gifts for transforming realities through empathy, accountability and care.

Empowering teams according to skills and purpose connecting actions to values experienced together from places of humility, appreciation and care for humanity's capacity for resilience above all else.

Authentic interaction fortifies integrity guiding words aligning with empowerment of communities' inherent worth navigated sincerely as equally respected partners confronting society's challenges collectively from within.

Motivating teams sustainably emerges from consistent care, compassion and appreciation recognizing humanity's shared experiences and imperfect yet invaluable wisdoms navigating complexities as companions, not directives alone.

Formative influences risked detachment through image versus humility and empowerment according organizing skills, livelihoods and visions for justice actualized cooperatively. Transitioning demands dismantling such silos through appeals to fellowship across perceived divides.

For too long, systems privileged directives detached from realities navigated thoughtfully from grassroots.

Wisdom surfaces prioritizing relationship-building through care, empathy and empowerment of communities' ownership over movement visions according organizing skills, experiences and shared purpose for dignity envisioned sincerely together.

Progress centered appeals to humanity's capacity for resilience through understanding above isolated agendas potentially widening disempowerment.

Consistency involves recognizing every person's imperfection as an opportunity for cultivating humility, growth and care through transparent yet compassionate accountability.

Formative experiences risks detachment through image alone versus empowering teams according lived experiences navigating tradeoffs thoughtfully alongside one another. Transitioning emerges dismantling such detachment by fortifying integrity through consistent appreciation, empathy and fellowship across perceived barriers uniting shared experiences confronting society's injustices collectively.

Authentic leaders motivate sustainably through compassionately acknowledging humanity's shared capacity for wisdom and resilience navigating complexities courageously together above directives alone. Challenges surfaced opportunities for cultivating humility and relationships empowering purpose beyond positions energizing teams according organizing skills and visions for justice experienced sincerely as respected companions journeying adversities as one dignified family.

Consistency empowered shared humanity experienced cooperatively above attributes dividing communities alone.

While inspiring sustainable impact proves profoundly challenging, authentic leadership emerges through nurturing connections empowering shared purpose navigated thoughtfully together. Consistency demands dismantling divides through appeals to humanity's shared experiences, capacity for wisdom and care across perceived barriers.

For example, recognizing excellence involves providing constructive yet compassionate feedback emphasizing progress made through cooperation instead of individualism. Formative influences risked detachment overlooking cooperation's gifts for the difficult road ahead journeyed courageously alongside one another. Transitioning dismantled such silos through care, empathy and appreciation of shared successes navigated sincerely as equally valued companions.

Similarly, cultivating understanding demands listening to understand diverse perspectives as equally valid through discernment instead of dismissal. Early focus risked detachment prioritizing fleeting perceptions over fellowship navigating tradeoffs thoughtfully together from places beyond differences alone. Transitioning emerged empowering shared purpose through care, humility and appeal to humanity's capacity for resilience surfacing where directives divide.

Furthermore, collaboration strengthens when leaders participate vulnerably and appreciate each contribution however imperfect. Formative experiences risked detachment preferring image over consistency fortifying integrity through care, accountability and compassion across perceived barriers uniting shared experiences confronting society's challenges collectively.

Transitioning dismantles such divides prioritizing whole wellbeing through fellowship.

4.2   Embracing diverse perspectives and fostering inclusiveness

While inspiring teams proves profoundly challenging, authentic leadership emerges through cultivating spaces where all people feel respected according to their shared humanity above perceived differences dividing alone.

Sustaining impact necessitates dismantling obstacles to dignity proposed through consistent care, empathy and appeal to fellowship experienced sincerely together confronting society's obstacles courageously as one dignified family.

Formative experiences risked detachment through directives disconnected from realities navigated thoughtfully from grassroots.

Transitioning demands consistency fortifying integrity by nurturing environments where diversity felt heard,

valued and empowered to contribute skills beyond surface attributes alone. Wisdom recognizes each person's imperfect yet invaluable gifts cultivated through relationship-building navigating tradeoffs compassionately alongside one another.

The empowerment of shared purpose through embracing varied perspectives as equally valid insights strengthening movements cooperatively.

Authentic interaction surfaces bringing diverse lived experiences together navigating tensions courageously with care, humility and appeal to humanity's capacity for understanding above all else.

Leadership emerges cultivating inclusive spaces encouraging empowerment of communities' inherently invaluable wisdoms for transforming society navigated sincerely together.

Consistency emerges dismantling divides privileging few detached voices potentially missing diversity of knowledge mobilizing shared purpose cooperatively.

Formative influences risks detachment through perceptions alone versus empowering grassroots networks as equally respected companions confronting obstacles to dignity envisioned collectively. Transitioning demands nurturing fellowship across perceived barriers united in care, accountability and courage to face society's challenges from within.

Inspiring positive change through inclusiveness proves challenging, authentic leadership emerges cultivating spaces where humanity's shared experiences feel empowered according to skills above outward attributes dividing alone.

Formative experiences risked detachment disempowering ownership of visions navigated thoughtfully together. Transitioning dismantles such divides through consistency fortifying integrity via care, empathy and appeal to fellowship.

For example, soliciting diverse input strengthens strategies navigating uncertainties collectively instead of directives potentially missing nuances.

Formative influences risked clinging to perceptions alone versus humility empowering wisdoms of grassroots networks navigating tradeoffs compassionately alongside one another.

Transitioning centers empowering shared purpose through relationships recognizing no individual alone arrives perfectly but through community.

Similarly, allocating roles and resources justly according to skills above perceptions strengthens morale and resilience confronting obstacles sincerely as respected companions. Early focus risked disempowerment detaching strategies from realities navigated thoughtfully from lived experiences.

Wisdom surfaces transitioning focus towards cultivating environments where people organize efforts according to strengths, yet imperfect visions for justice experienced cooperately.

Furthermore, prioritizing equitable accommodations so all may contribute fully dismantles barriers to participation. Formative experiences risked excluding voices missing diversity of invaluable wisdoms mobilizing shared purpose through fellowship.

Transitioning emerges empowering grassroots networks navigating differences courageously together from humility instead of directives alone.

Consistency emerges dismantling divides through appeals to humanity's shared capacity for understanding above attributes dividing people alone.

Authentic leaders embrace varied perspectives recognizing no individual alone arrives perfectly, but through humility, care and cooperation navigating tradeoffs compassionately alongside one another as equally respected companions on the challenging road ahead.

Our common experiences risked detachment disempowering ownership of transforming society according to skills, not perceptions organizing efforts thoughtfully together. Transitioning surfaces empowering purpose through relationships across perceived barriers united in confront society's adversities courageously from within through appeals to shared humanity.

4.3 Empowering others and creating a safe space for learning

Nurturing human connection proves profoundly complex, authentic leadership emerges through empowering shared purpose navigated thoughtfully together from grassroots. Formative influences risked detachment through directives alone versus cultivating fellowship where all feel respected to contribute imperfect yet invaluable wisdoms. Transitioning surfaces dismantling such divides consistently fortifying integrity through care, empathy and appeals to humanity.

This subchapter explores leadership lessons gleaned emphasizing empowerment according to skills beyond attributes dividing alone. Authentic interaction emerges bringing lived experiences together navigating uncertainties sincerely with humility, accountability and care for shared humanity's capacity for understanding above all else.

Empowering spaces encourages participation from networked wisdoms strengthening liberation visions cooperatively confronted challenges courageously as equally respected companions.

Consistency demands recognizing no individual alone arrives perfectly but through open-mindedness, cooperation and care for one another above transient positions. Formative experiences risked passivity versus nurturing forums where grassroots networks organize efforts navigating tradeoffs thoughtfully from lived realities united in confront society's obstacles sincerely as one dignified family. Transitioning dismantles such divides empowering shared purpose through relationships.

For example, cultivating skills emerges transferring not only methods but ownership of liberating movements according lived wisdoms navigated earnestly together from grassroots. Early focus risked detachment disempowering communities' resilience and visions for justice experienced cooperately.

Wisdom surfaces transitioning strategic focus towards empowering diversity of invaluable voices united in navigating uncertainties courageously through care, accountability and appeal to fellowship.
Similarly, empowering leadership potential involves championing varied perspectives through equitable support and resources recognizing no singular path arrives perfectly, but sincerely through cooperation navigating complexities compassionately alongside one another.

Formative influences risked limiting possibilities disempowering communities determining allocation according strengths organized thoughtfully together.

Transitioning dismantles such silos empowering grassroots networks' ownership over movements visioned cooperatively.

Furthermore, empowering independence strengthens resilience confronting obstacles courageously from grassroots through guidance instead of directives potentially limiting diversity of skills mobilized cooperatively.

Early focus risked passivity versus establishing spaces where people felt respected navigating tradeoffs earnestly according lived experiences.
Transitioning surfaced transitioning focus towards empowering shared purpose through relationships across perceived differences.

Consistency fortifies integrity through transparent yet caring accountability navigated willingly alongside one another. Formative experiences risked disempowering grassroots networks' commitment mobilizing shared humanity above transient divides alone.

Transitioning dismantles such barriers nurturing safe spaces where people felt encouraged pursuing purposes united navigating adversities boldly yet sincerely together as respected companions on the journey ahead.

Empowering others proves profoundly complex, authentic leadership emerges cultivating spaces where communities feel respected determining visions and strategies navigated earnestly from grassroots.

Formative experiences risked detachment through unilateral directives versus empowering shared purpose experienced cooperatively. Transitioning dismantles such silos through consistency upholding integrity via fellowship.

For example, acknowledging interdependence strengthens commitment navigating uncertainties courageously together instead of isolationism. Early focus risked detachment through individualism versus empowering grassroots networks' ownership over transforming society thoughtfully alongside one another.

Wisdom surfaces reorienting focus towards cooperation recognizing humanity's shared experiences confronting injustices collectively.

Similarly, validating identities fortifies spirits resiliently facing challenges sincerely as equally valued companions. Formative influences risked exclusion disempowering diversity of invaluable wisdoms empowering shared purpose experienced cooperatively.

Transitioning dismantles such divides centering appeals to humanity's capacity for understanding navigating complexities compassionately as one dignified family.

Furthermore, encouragingExperimentation fosters innovation surfacing where directives limit resilience navigating obstacles boldly yet sincerely alongside one another. Early influences risked passivity versus establishing spaces encouraging people exploring approaches navigating uncertainties thoughtfully from grassroots.

Transitioning dismantles such barriers nurturing safe havens where communities felt secure organizing efforts earnestly as companions on the difficult road ahead.

Moreover, cultivating dignity through respectful dissent defuses tensions cooperatively navigating differences courageously together instead of directives alone. Formative experiences risked discord through distant views absent fellowship.

Wisdom surfaces transitioning focus towards humility recognizing no singular perspective alone arrives perfectly, but through cooperation navigating uncertainties sincerely alongside one another.

Authentic leaders empower shared purpose through relationships built on care, empathy and appeals to humanity's shared capacity for understanding navigating complexities courageously together above fleeting attributes dividing communities alone.

Formative influences risked detachment versus consistency fortifying integrity via empowering grassroots networks' ownership over transforming realities envisioned cooperatively. Transitioning dismantles divides through fellowship.

4.4 Cultivating the next generation of authentic leaders

While nurturing future leadership proves profoundly challenging, authenticity emerges through empowering shared purpose navigated thoughtfully together. Formative experiences risked detachment through directives versus cultivating spaces encouraging successors respected equally according skills above attributes dividing alone. Transitioning demands consistency fortifying integrity via care, humility and empowerment of grassroots networks.

Strengthening grassroots successors navigating uncertainties courageously alongside one another through transparent yet compassionate mentoring nurturing dignity envisioned cooperatively.

Authentic interaction surfaces bringing lived experiences together navigating tensions sincerely with accountability and care for humanity's capacity to understand navigating complexities as respected companions. Empowering spaces fosters leadership potential beyond any positional title.

For example, transferring skills involves championing diversity of invaluable wisdoms strengthened through fellowship above perceptions dividing alone. Early focus risked disempowering successors navigating tradeoffs earnestly from places empowering ownership over shared purpose.

Transitioning dismantles such barriers nurturing environments encouraging successors exploring approaches courageously together as valued companions.

Similarly, cultivating empathy necessitates walking uncertainties navigated thoughtfully together instead of separating positional titles potentially constricting equitable support.

Formative influences risk risked detaching mentees navigating adversities resiliently from grassroots. Wisdom surfaces reorienting focus towards fellowship where successors felt empowered determining strategies cooperatively from lived experiences.

Furthermore, nurturing autonomy empowers innovation traversing obstacles boldly yet sincerely together. Early focus risked directives limiting successors' ownership of transforming society envisioned cooperatively. Transitioning dismantles such silos through establishing spaces encouraging successors navigating tensions courageously guided yet empowered according organizing skills thoughtfully from grassroots.

Consistency demands recognition of humanity's imperfection arriving cooperatively through caring accountability navigated willingly together from places beyond fleeting attributes dividing people alone.

Formative experiences risked limiting ownership disempowering grassroots networks envisioning newer approaches navigated earnestly as respected companions. Transitioning dismantles barriers through empowering shared purpose experienced cooperatively.

Empowering future leaders proves profoundly challenging, authenticity emerges cultivating spaces where successors feel respected navigating complexities courageously together. Wisdom recognizes arriving imperfectly yet through cooperation instead of directives alone potentially limiting equity. Transitioning dismantles divides through appeals to shared humanity.

For example, acknowledging interdependence strengthens resilience confronting obstacles sincerely as respected companions instead of individualism.

Formative influences risked disempowering successors' ownership of transforming society thoughtfully together from grassroots. Transitioning emerges empowering networks navigating differences cooperatively through care, humility and fellowship.

Similarly, validating identities fortifies spirits resiliently facing uncertainties as equally valued friends.

Early focus risked exclusion disempowering diversity of invaluable skills empowering shared purpose experienced cooperatively.

Transitioning dismantles barriers centering humanity's capacity for understanding navigating complexities compassionately as one dignified family.

Furthermore, encouraging experimentation fosters holistic growth surfacing where directives single out successors navigating tradeoffs thoughtfully through networks instead. Formative experiences risked detachment versus empathy and care establishing spaces where successors felt empowered exploring approaches guided yet freely according organizing skills and purpose.

Moreover, cultivating dignity through respect cultivates understanding navigating differences courageously together instead of dividing alone. Wisdom surfaces reorienting towards humility, recognizing no singular view alone transforms perfectly, but through relationships of care, accountability and fellowship across perceived barriers united in navigating society's challenges collectively.

Additionally, establishing equity involves allocating resources and opportunities justly according to skills and strengths above fleeting attributes potentially limiting grassroots leadership potential.

Transitioning dismantles such silos through nurturing environments where successors felt motivated and supported navigating complexities courageously from lived experiences.

Consistency emerges empowering shared progress navigated thoughtfully together through caring accountability ensuring successors voice matters equally alongside others as respected companions on the journey ahead.

Formative experiences risked detachment versus integrity fortified by empowering grassroots networks envisioning change earnestly cooperatively.

Chapter 05

Sustaining Authentic Impact Over Time

Leadership demands not only cultivating trust through vulnerability, but fortifying authentic connections sustainably over time amid inevitable change.

However, maintaining coherence proves challenging as realities shift and new priorities emerge risking disconnect between principles and actions.

Consistency requires persevering integrity by consistently navigating tradeoffs with care, wisdom and community.

For too long, early ambitions emphasized image over substance alone, risking impact fading when pressures mounted. Formative experiences conditioned worth through fleeting validation instead of lasting change. Transitioning demanded transitioning away from directives and towards relationship-building sustainably empowering purpose.

Maintaining credibility long-term necessitates authenticity connecting rhetoric with humanity's shared capacity for resilience through cooperation.
This chapter explores my ongoing evolution fortifying meaningful impact through consistency navigating complexities together from grassroots.

Early, over-extending risks burnout disconnecting actions from why work matters most deeply.

Transitioning involved cultivating balanced, empathetic yet bold leadership fortifying purpose through self-care, accountability and appeal to shared service.

Sustaining authentic relationships long-term necessitates persevering integrity guided by justice, empathy and hope.

Consistency requires navigating tradeoffs thoughtfully amid pressures towards expediency alone. For example, certain initiatives faced tensions between speed and inclusion necessitating recalibration through collaborative problem-solving.

Acknowledging limitations invited joint navigation of uncertainties from places of learning instead of directives alone. Progress centered appeals to our interdependent humanity.

Furthermore, sustaining impact involves cultivating spaces where communities felt empowered leading sustainably from within. Early, performative strengths undermined integrity through compliance alone instead of dignity.

Transitioning demanded dismantling obstacles so that all people experienced liberation proposed without fear of reprisal. Consistency emerged recognizing no experience inherently superior, though differing, within our shared journey.

Leadership lessons arose not from arriving flawlessly but authentically navigating complexities with humility, care and community. For example, acknowledging miscalculations strengthened strategies through collective wisdom versus isolated reactions. Initiatives strengthened from listening to needs of those directly impacted, not removed directives potentially missing nuances. Progress centered dignity and fellowship above unilateral control.

Sustaining impact long-term requires persevering integrity guided by justice, empathy and appeal to humanity's shared capacity for resilience.

When rhetoric matches living respectfully, consistency emerges empowering purpose through cooperation confronting challenges together from grassroots as equals. Our shared experiences call leaders to build and walk alongside communities with candor, accountability and hope.

5.1   Adapting to challenges while staying true to principles

Maintaining coherence amid inevitable change proves demanding, requiring wisdom navigating tensions sincerely yet constructively. For too long, early leadership succumbed to pressures divorcing actions from guiding ethics of justice and care for community.

Transitioning demanded recognizing no path arrived perfectly, but surfaced through cooperation facing challenges together from within.

Practice emerged transitioning towards dignity and fellowship instead of directives alone. Certain pivots adjusted strategies while reaffirming purpose through collaborative problem-solving versus reaction. For example, acknowledgements navigating initiatives imperfectly taught humility prioritizing learning through open dialogue over defensiveness potentially undermining integrity. Progress centered appeals to shared values of liberation for all.

Consistency surfaced transitioning away from performative strengths disconnected from realities towards relationship-building sustainably empowering purpose.

Challenges proved opportunities dismantling obstacles through appeals to our interdependence and capacity for resilience.

Early pressures emphasized technical fixes disconnected from humanity's varied yet equally valuable wisdoms requiring integration cooperatively.

For example, acknowledging limitations where certain initiatives faced tensions between speed and inclusion invited jointly recalibrating proportionately and strategizing inclusively.

Our shared experiences navigating life's struggles called for navigating tradeoffs with care, empathy and recognition of perspectives historically marginalized within movements. Progress centered appeals to fellowship above unilateral directives.

Similarly, candidly sharing hardships like burnout and pandemic-induced stress normalized struggles as universal rather than personal failures.

Guiding empathetic conversations modeled resolving tensions constructively by appealing to purpose and shared capacity for growth within community instead of isolated complaints.

Consistency emerged navigating uncertainties together compassionately through humility and care for all people.

Maintaining coherence amid change necessitates persevering integrity guided by justice, empathy and appeal to shared service. When rhetoric matches sincerely embracing complexity, adaptability emerges empowering sustained purpose through cooperation confronted challenges collectively from within as equally dignified partners. Our shared humanity calls leaders to build and walk alongside communities with candor, accountability and hope.

While change proves inevitable, sustaining impact long-term requires persevering integrity through consistency navigating tradeoffs authentically with community.

Formative experiences risked dismissing dissent as disloyalty instead of opportunities for growth.

Transitioning demanded cultivating spaces where differences felt respected through appeals to fellowship rather than directives alone. Receptiveness to critiques, though inconvenient, meant addressing underlying interests and correcting course jointly from shared purpose.

For example, acknowledging blind spots where complacency clouded objective analysis invited cooperative exploration of solutions strengthening accountability.

Progress centered guided discussions focusing motivations driving valid concerns and proposing remedies collaboratively through empathy.

Similarly, candid reflections on miscalculations or unintended harms normalized struggles as opportunities for learning together versus personal failings. Consistency emerged jointly navigating uncertainties with care, wisdom and recognition of diverse stakeholders' needs to reform with dignity for all.

Leadership lessons involved authentically embracing complexity navigated with communities, not despite them.

Initiatives strengthened from trusting directly impacted people's lived experiences rather than removed prescriptions risking tokenism or paternalism. Progress centered grassroots empowerment.

Challenges proved chances for growth dismantling silos through relationships across perceived differences.

Early responses fixated individual advancement disconnected from purpose empowering marginalized through cooperation instead of directives alone.

Transitioning nurtured diversity of voices elevating fellowship above preconceptions.

Sustaining authentic impact long-term necessitates persevering integrity guided by justice, empathy and appeals to humanity's shared capacity for resilience. When facing difficulties, consistency emerges navigating tradeoffs respectfully through wisdom, humility and care for community as equally dignified partners. Our common experiences call leaders to build and walk alongside communities as learners, not authority alone.

5.2   Maintaining self-awareness through reflection and growth

Sustaining meaningful impact long-term demands navigating inevitable change authentically through ongoing introspection and accountability. However, maintaining objectivity proves challenging when pressures mount requiring transition away from isolated efforts towards relationship-building.

Formative experiences risked conditioning worth through image management alone instead of growth. Transitioning emerged dismantling performative strengths through candid self-assessment and willingness to recognize limitations from places of shared learning. Early barriers fixated on perceptions of perfection instead of imperfect progress navigated sincerely with community.

Practice involved cultivating spaces where communities felt respected and differences strengthened fellowship rather than compliance.

Leadership lessons centered authentically embracing complexity through guidance from grassroots solutions directly addressing needs, not removed directives potentially missing nuances of lived experiences. Progress emerged from humility and cooperation instead of directives alone.

For example, certain critiques faced instinctive defenses necessitating patience and care to understand diverse perspectives as equally valid through discernment versus division.

Consistency surfaced navigating ambiguities sincerely and courageously alongside one another through empathy, accountability and care.

Addressing struggles holistically without defensiveness centered appeals to shared purpose over isolated agendas.

Furthermore, authentic reflection dismantled obstacles through receptive problem-solving across perceived differences.

Early resistance to feedback risked deepening divides versus unity in growth. Transitioning emerged recognizing no perspective inherently superior through fellowship rather than compliance.

Consistency involved candid self-assessment and willingness to correct course jointly from shared values.

Maintaining self-awareness also meant modeling health through balance instead of martyrdom. Formative experiences conditioned worth through exhaustion unsustainable for purpose outliving individuals.

Transitioning demanded prioritizing downtime and care for whole selves through humbled appreciation of limitations and interdependence. Progress centered embracing help as strength, not failure alone.

Sustaining coherence amid change necessitates ongoing introspection fortifying integrity guided by justice, empathy and appeal to humanity's shared capacity for understanding. When facing difficulties, authenticity emerges navigating tradeoffs respectfully through candor, humility and care for community as equally respected partners. Our shared experiences call leaders to build and walk alongside communities as learners, not authority alone.

While sustaining impact long-term proves challenging, wisdom demands maintaining objectivity navigating complexities sincerely with community. Formative experiences risked clinging to perceived strengths instead of humility and growth. Transitioning involved cultivating spaces where communities felt empowered strengthening fellowship through shared experiences.

For example, periodic partnership built trust for candid yet caring evaluations dismantling perceived barriers to progress together. Conversations centered cooperative problem-solving versus personalized critiques through empathy and care for shared humanity. Accountability emerged empowering purpose beyond temporary positions alone through cooperation.

Similarly, reflections on missteps transitioned from defensive reactions towards collective strategizing recognizing potential harms as learning opportunities. Consistency surfaced navigating differences humbly and respectfully alongside one another through openness and compassion.
Addressing limitations jointly centered appeals to justice, wisdom and care.

Furthermore, taking time for self-care like sabbaticals modeled balancing demands sustainably without martyrdom. Early resistance risked deprioritizing rest unsustainable for longevity in service. Transitioning recognized no path perfectly arrived, but required navigating tradeoffs together sincerely through interdependence and care for whole communities' welfare above isolation.

Maintaining self-awareness invites discerning needs calmly through input across perceived divides. When facing challenges, authenticity emerges cooperatively navigating complexities respectfully as equally respected partners. The shared experiences of all of us call leaders to engage communities as learners alongside instead of authority alone through candor and care. Together, integrity perseveres sustainably.

5.3 Leaving a meaningful and enduring cultural legacy

Sustaining authentic impact long-term involves more than navigating change through consistency and self-awareness alone. True leadership emerges empowering purpose outliving any individual by dismantling obstacles through community. However, fortifying lasting change proves challenging amid inevitable transitions necessitating wisdom navigating possibilities thoughtfully.

Formative experiences risked prioritizing fleeting gains and image alone instead of structural reforms ensuring liberation proposed endured for generations.

Transitioning demanded shifting towards empowering grassroots movements sustainably from within through cooperation and appeal to shared humanity. For too long, directives risked weakening longevity of movements by disempowering communities' ownership of visions actualized from their lived realities and needs.

Consistency emerged transitioning away from directives and towards relationship-building fortifying visions through communities' resilience, leadership and wisdom navigating tradeoffs sincerely together over time.

Early barriers fixation on isolated actions risked purpose fading when perceived supporters departed versus empowerment anchored dignity of all people. Progress centered appeals to fellowship above unilateral control potentially undermining integrity through compliance alone.

Cultivating spaces where those directly impacted felt heard strengthened dignity despite differences in outward demographics.

Formative experiences conditioned deference to perceived authority risking movements crippled or co-opted without communities fully empowered leading according to their visions and strengths. Transitioning demanded dismantling obstacles so that liberating proposals felt owned from ground up through grassroots cooperation.

For example, cultivating next generation leadership through mentorship transferred skills and commitment to structural reforms outliving any single advocate.

Consistency surfaced empowering purpose beyond temporary positions alone through cooperative strategizing, capacity-building and fellowship across perceived barriers towards shared humanity above attributes dividing.

Progress centered empowering grassroots networks over directives potentially disconnecting strategies from realities.

Similarly, allocating resources through participatory decision-making processes rooted visions in realities navigating tradeoffs thoughtfully and justly according to communities' wisdom versus removed perceptions.

Authentic forums dismantled hierarchical structures transitioning towards distributed leadership strengthening ownership, networks and resilience navigating uncertainties collectively from within. Shared purpose united empowering diversity of voices organizing according to skills and uniquely impacting realities.

Overall, leaving meaningful legacies involves fortifying liberating visions beyond individuals through relationship-building consistently empowering grassroots networks as equally respected partners navigating together cooperatively.

When rhetoric aligns with sincerely embracing complexity navigated jointly from ground up through fellowship, structural reforms proposed outlive advocates through communities' ownership, wisdom and perseverance confronting adversities collectively. Our shared humanity calls leaders to develop along with, not apart from, those directly impacted sustain empowerment for all people now and future generations navigating life's shared struggles and potential for justice as one dignified family.

While sustaining impact long-term proves profoundly challenging, authentic leadership emerges empowering purpose through dismantling obstacles to liberation envisioned by movements from grassroots. Formative experiences risked prioritizing isolated directives alone instead of community empowerment ensuring visions actualized justly endured.

Transitioning demanded shifting focus towards relationship-building fortifying structural reforms through grassroots resilience and wisdom navigating tradeoffs collectively over generations.

Early barriers of hierarchical directives risked weakening diversity of networks owning visions from lived realities navigated with care, empathy and fellowship instead of unilateral control.

For example, cultivating next generation leadership involved supporting communities according organizing their skills, lived experiences and visions for beloved communities instead of directives potentially detaching strategies from those most impacted.

Consistency surfaced navigating differences respectfully through appeals to shared humanity above perceived divides of attributes alone.

Similarly, allocating resources through participatory processes empowered grassroots networks determining allocation according to realities navigated with communities instead of isolated perceptions potentially missing nuances.

Formats dismantled top-down structures by transitioning leadership towards diversity of voices united in shared purpose of justice, empathy and care for people empowering visions outlived individuals.

Furthermore, building infrastructure like training spaces and legal defense funds supported liberation efforts organized according to grassroots wisdom navigating political realities cooperatively. Early resistance risked weakening sustainability of movements without equipping communities navigating challenges collectively as equally respected partners. Transitioning recognized no single path perfectly arrived, but emerged through relationship-building.

Consistently fortifying movements in this way transitioned focus from isolated gains towards empowering visions proposed endured through networks, resilience and fellowship navigating tradeoffs sincerely from ground up.

Formative experiences risked prioritizing perceived supporters alone instead of structural reforms ensuring liberation visions proposed endured for all people through grassroots ownership, diversity and care. Transitioning emerged empowering dignity for humanity above attributes dividing.

Leaving meaningful legacies emerges through relationship-building fortifying purpose beyond individuals by empowering grassroots networks navigating tradeoffs thoughtfully according to lived wisdoms, skills and visions for justice as equally respected partners.

When rhetoric matches sincerely embracing complexity navigated cooperatively, structural reforms proposed outlive advocates through communities' ownership of their shared humanity's capacity for understanding above attributes dividing.

5.4 Call to action for readers to step into authentic leadership

Sustaining authentic impact demands more than navigating change alone - it requires cultivating the next generation of leaders empowered in their own journeys. However, stepping into one's highest purpose proves challenging amid pressures towards isolation and expediency.
Wisdom emerges nurturing spaces where skills feel developed through community.
Formative experiences risked prioritizing image over substance disconnected from purpose beyond fleeting wins. Transitioning calls recognizing no path arrives perfectly, but surfaces through relationship-building.

Early focus on directives alone risked detachment from realities navigated jointly from grassroots. Consistency demands dismantling such barriers through appeals to fellowship.

A call to action for readers to step boldly into their leadership journey empowered from lived wisdoms and skills, not removed directives potentially missing nuances of experiences.

Humanity calls nurturing each other in courageously confronting society's obstacles together from within.

For too long systems privileged few voices while marginalizing others, necessitating transition towards distributing leadership according to shared purpose of justice, empathy and care for people in their diversity.

Formative conditions risked passivity instead of stepping boldly alongside communities navigating tradeoffs thoughtfully from grassroots. Wisdom emerges embracing complexities through open-mindedness and goodwill.

Consistency emerges cultivating spaces where all people experience liberation proposed as equally respected partners navigating differences humbly and courageously together.

Fellowship dismantles silos of "us vs them" transitioning focus towards shared endeavors confronting adversities through understanding across perceived barriers. Progress centers appeals to humanity above fleeting positions dividing alone.

For example, acknowledging each person's uniquely valuable yet imperfect wisdoms strengthens collective strategizing dismantling obstacles to dignity envisioned cooperatively from lived experiences. Similarly, cultivating skills through mentorship transfers methods navigating tensions sincerely alongside one another with care, patience and care for people in their diversity above quick resolutions alone.

Readers, I implore you to step boldly yet humbly into your leadership potential through relationship-building from grassroots as respected partners confronting society's obstacles to justice.

Our common stories navigating life's struggles call us to walk courageously alongside one another dismantling divides empowering dignity for people in their diversity above attributes dividing alone.
Kindness, courage and care for shared humanity's capacity for resilience can propel progress where directives fall short.

You possess uniquely valuable yet imperfect insights strengthening movements through empathy, accountability and fellowship across perceived differences.

Step courageously with communities navigating uncertainties thoughtfully from lived wisdoms, skills and care for shared humanity above fleeting positions alone disconnecting actions from purpose.

Together, sustaining authentic impact emerges empowering dignity through consistency facing society's challenges sincerely as one dignified family. We come to a common ground, surfaces wisdom recognizing no individual arrives perfectly, but gleans insights navigating tradeoffs compassionately alongside one another.

Step boldly yet humbly into authentic leadership emancipating purpose through empowering grassroots resilience, ownership and care for shared humanity above attributes dividing people alone. Kindness, courage and fellowship can dismantle obstacles where directives fall short.

This call to step boldly into one's leadership reflects lessons navigating complexities is a lifelong journey best traveled sincerely alongside others.

While finding courage proves demanding, sustaining authentic impact emerges through cultivating spaces where communities feel empowered according to skills and livelihoods navigated thoughtfully from grassroots.

Formative experiences risked clinging to perceptions alone versus humility and growth. Transitioning emerged dismantling such silos through relationship-building across perceived divides. Readers, trust that every interaction presents chances for fellowship recognizing shared experiences confronting society's challenges collectively.

For too long, passive acceptance privileged few directing movements from removed theories potentially detached from realities navigated jointly.

Wisdom surfaces transitioning focus towards empowering grassroots networks through guidance from lived wisdoms navigating tradeoffs sincerely together instead of directives alone. Progress centers enabling dignity proposed as envisioned cooperatively from ground up.

For example, acknowledging imperfection as opportunity for learning strengthens movements navigating differences respectfully through empathy, accountability and care for shared humanity above fleeting attributes dividing alone.

Cultivating skills emerges from mentoring to transfer not only methods but commitment to justice, wisdom and empowering success of endeavors according to skills and visions for beloved communities envisioned cooperatively.

Leading authentically also requires prioritizing whole well-being to avoid burnout through sustainable balance. Formative influences risked worth through exhaustion alone.

Transitioning emerges dismantling such barriers by cultivating fellowship as nourishment for challenges ahead journeyed cooperatively instead of directives potentially detaching strategies from realities navigated thoughtfully from grassroots.

Readers, courage surfaces through humility, open-mindedness and relationship-building across perceived divides facing society's obstacles sincerely as one dignified family.

I implore embracing complexities navigated gently and courageously alongside others according to lived experiences, not fleeting perceptions potentially missing diversity of invaluable wisdoms strengthened movements through fellowship above all.

Our humanity calls nurturing each other in confronting adversities boldly yet respectfully as equally valued partners instead of directives potentially disempowering grassroots ownership of transforming realities.

Every interaction presents chances for empowering dignity through fellowship, accountability and care.

Kindness, empathy and enabling success of all people surfaces where directives fall short. You possess invaluable yet imperfect gifts for justice - now go and step courageously.

***

Note from the Author:

I have sought to share the profound lessons I have learned on my own journey toward more authentic leadership. Through candid reflections on both my successes and failures, I aim to demonstrate for readers how cultivating integrity, consistency and genuine human connection are vital for any leader hoping to create lasting change.

Time and again, I have found that true leadership emerges not from directives or image alone, but from the ability to dismantle obstacles in a way that empowers others according to their own skills and wisdom. My goal in penning these stories and strategies is to equip others with the tools to align their rhetoric with reality, to navigate tensions with communities rather than apart from them, and to mobilize positive change through inspiring shared purpose rather than compliance.

The transformative power of which I write comes not from any singular experience, but from a lifelong commitment to self-awareness, accountability and relationship-building across perceived differences. Through humility, empathy and care for humanity's capacity for understanding above all else, we can overcome even the most deeply entrenched challenges. It is my hope that readers draw encouragement from these examples and insights, finding the courage to step boldly yet sincerely into their own leadership roles through empowering grassroots networks as respected partners on the journey.

If my personal evolution illustrates anything, it is that we all possess invaluable gifts and blind spots - and authentic progress emerges cooperatively over individual arrivals. May this work support many more in cultivating consistency, coherence and compassion, that together we might empower dignity for all people through fellowship, wisdom and relentless care for one another.

About the Author:

Mustafa A. Nejem is a maritime visionary with a captain's heart and an island soul. In his island home, the sea's love, sailing's legacy, and leadership's flame passed down through generations with pride and glory. He is a skilled navigator of words, charting a course through the vast ocean of knowledge. With his expertise and passion, he guides readers towards prosperous shores, unveiling the secrets of maritime life and business success in concise and captivating prose.

www.ingramcontent.com/pod-product-compliance
Lightning Source LLC
Chambersburg PA
CBHW080851120626
46546CB00008B/2780